Madonna Fans Do It Better
a FANthology about the Queen of Pop

Copyright © 2021 Tookman Productions
All rights reserved.
ISBN: 978-0-578-34514-7

Madonna Fans Do It Better
a FANthology about the Queen of Pop

Editors, LeeAnn Tooker and Heather Turman

Foreword by Heather Matarazzo

Authors:
Faye Rapoport DesPres
Lisa Gopman
Saima Huq
Teddy Margas
Nick Musmecci
Tommy Natoli
Matthew Nouriel
Lawrence Stern
LeeAnn Tooker
Heather Turman
Denise Bella Vlasis
Patricia White

FOREWORD
by Heather Matarazzo

When I was asked to write the foreword of this book my first thought was, "What could be said about Madonna that hasn't been said already?" Almost every word in every language has been used to describe her, some more eloquent than others. Visionary, demon, goddess, Satan, whore, saint, sinner, priestess, cheap, priceless... you get the gist. Like so many others throughout the world Madonna has influenced my life in ways no other artist has.

As one gets older, it can be hard to distinguish which memories are one's own, versus the memories one appropriates from stories told by others. I was a child of the 80's, raised in a home by parents who were not mine biologically. I came to them through the foster care system at the age of two and was adopted a few years later. One of the stories they used to tell repeatedly was how I didn't speak for almost a year after I was placed in their care and made no facial expressions. However, that all changed on the day when I saw Madonna for the first time on TV. I remember distinctly sitting on our brown carpet in the den, as close to the TV as my mother would allow and experiencing what can only be described as a transcendent experience -- it was a recorded concert of the "Like a Virgin" tour. Madonna appeared on stage wearing a sparkly jacket of some kind and started singing "Dress You Up". I pointed to the TV and uttered my first words, "I do that". In one moment, she helped me discover my voice. And I haven't stopped using it since.

That is not only the mark of a brilliant artist but a brilliant being. In her continual demonstration of being true to herself, standing up for what is right, even in the midst of criticism and ostracism, she has given other people the empowerment to do the same. She has reminded us that we are the ones we have always been waiting for and that we don't need anyone's permission to be who we are. And for that, we love her. This book reflects those sentiments; a collection of stories that show just how much of a life empowering source Madonna has been for so many and it is my honor to introduce said book to you now.

From one Madonna fan to another,
Heather Matarazzo

CONTENTS

1	House of Integrity	3
2	Madonna in My Life	11
3	A Girl Who Loved to Dance	17
4	My Madonna Story	27
5	My Madonna	33
6	And You Can Dance, For Inspiration…	39
7	Borderline	47
8	Madonna Moments	55
9	The Art of Being a Human Being	61
10	Feminique	71
11	Immaculate Connection	79
12	My Life As Madonna	87

"The history of women in popular music can, pretty much, be divided into before and after Madonna."

– Susan Sarandon

Vogue
Artist: Jacqueline Bissett
Website: JacquelineBissett.com

HOUSE OF INTEGRITY
by Tommy Natoli

     A Thanksgiving tradition in my home is to start prepping food early in the morning, turn on NBC for the Macy's parade, and then of course watch Madonna's 1990 documentary *Truth or Dare*. One might question the relevance of this film on America's special day, but to me every time I reflect on my life and experiences of the past, my gratitude will always include Madonna and the infinite contributions she has made to our culture and my life. The connection I have with her is deeper and more meaningful to me than your basic Instagram follower, fan, lamb, or whatever else people call themselves these days. On the day that is supposed to be about thankfulness, it is important for me to pay a small homage to the woman who saved so many of us from the pits of gay despair and self-loathing. At the height of her fame she used her mainstream platform to show support of marginalized communities at a time of extreme conservatism.

     Growing up my home was not the place I longed to be, it was not the haven it is for most people. I loved going to school and to friends' houses because for me, my bully lived at home and I was regularly berated for being a girly little boy. Constantly emasculated for my mannerisms and ideas, I was an over-the-top child, I loved singing and dancing and forever living in make believe magical fairy tale land. All those things soon became secret enjoyments of mine once I learned the deep sting of judgement. Madonna was a closeted hobby of mine because she was a gay icon so polarizing and controversial that admitting you liked her was the kiss of death in a small strait-laced working-class town. In a strange way you sort of have to come out as a Madonna fan, and the rare moments when you meet someone else that shares your love, it's like meeting a long-lost sibling you never knew about. I was only able to be myself when nobody was home, or I was alone in my room which as a latchkey kid of the nineties, was mostly all of the time.

In 1993 I was ten years old and figuring out the world, absorbing all the information basic cable television could pump into my little brain. Fascinated by pop culture and in love with listening to and recording my terrestrial radio, Madonna intrigued and confused me as a young child. Her constant changing image which set her above all her competitors made me feel like I was a detective putting together a story. "Ok so, the woman dancing in front of the burning cross, the lady in the material girl video, and the *Vogue* singer are all the same person, right?". Once I wrapped my head around what a makeover was, I was fascinated and fully captivated by this artist who was beautiful, glamorous and did not care what people thought of her. By the time I was a teenager it was a regular habit of mine to be down at the local Blockbuster Video checking out every Madonna concert in stock. God I was gay!

My best friend Kate and I were teenagers on the forefront of dial up technology and when her new computer came with a super high-tech DVD player, we immediately invested in purchasing *The Girlie Show* concert tour. Holy shit. Talk about life changing and some great jerking off material for this horned-up gay teenager! A simulated on-stage orgy with boys gyrating on top of each other not only unhinged my jaw from itself, but it also opened my eyes to an entire world of fabulous men doing whatever they wanted. I want to be *that* when I grow up! When I moved in with Kate and her Mom at fifteen years old, I was able for the first time to live in a state of self-expression. No longer contained to my bedroom, we lived on a cranberry farm with 88 acres of land that allowed me to put my headphones on and bop and dance around the dirt roads and woods pretending I was performing for thousands of fans on the *Blonde Ambition Tour*. We also used to get shit-tanked drunk on stolen cheap vodka and repeatedly watched the concert trying to learn the choreography.

As a high school student, the only things I liked were lunch time, drama club, and writing sassy papers in all my classes. When my tenth-grade English teacher would pull me aside and address the obscenities in my recent essay, I would tell her "I am an artist and this is how I choose to express myself, I can't change the paper because that would be compromising my artistic integrity." I negotiated with her that I could swear in my written assignments as my first amendment right, but I would be deducted points for every curse word used. I'm not changing my fucking show! It was more than just loving a pop star; it was knowing that this was the kind of person I wanted to be. Beyond the surface level bullshit of fame and fortune, I wanted to have her integrity and she made me want to be an artist because it seemed like great power. Nobody can take away your self-expression, your intention or whatever your mind creates. Art was power. Music was power. Words were power.

When I realized that you could carve out a life on this planet that revolved around creating and expressing what I was feeling on the inside, I was all in. Education and career planning that most people take on, deciding whether to go into law or medicine was never even a thought in my mind. For me it has nothing to do with catchy pop songs or great dancing, those are just awesome bonuses. I wanted to be an artist! Of course, her trailblazing advocacy for gay and human rights has been inspiring and life changing for millions of people all over the world. Beyond all the pedestrian facts we know of her and her phenomenal success, the true joy and beauty of this artist is that she can pick me up, lift me up from whatever dark depression I am in and wake me up. Whether it was when I was in the closet or out and proud, when I am alone and can put my air pods on, blast *Express Yourself* and dance around my home, I am free. I have a lifelong struggle with depression, anxiety, self-esteem, the whole works! Madonna's art helps shift my thinking, she has influenced me to keep going and to take care of myself.

Self-care is a struggle for me. I love taking a shower and listening to *Rain* from the *Erotica* album. It is so literal and cheesy, but it brings me back to being ten years old and hopeful for the future. When I am wanting to get pumped up I listen to one of the tour albums. When I have an important performance or presentation, I listen to *Vogue* beforehand, it centers my mind and gets me in a I'm-in-charge-and-glamourous state of mind. Sometimes I don't even know what mood I am in; I am unaware of how I feel exactly and I will get Madonna nudges. For example, randomly and suddenly I will need to hear *Causing a Commotion* but a specific live or remix version. Then I dive into it manically, and before I know it, I have listened to whatever has popped into my mind over and over for a week and I feel better, or I have figured out my problem, or my writer's block disappears.

My first Madonna concert was the 2004 *Reinvention Tour* in Worcester, MA and I got the cheapest nosebleed behind the stage seats. I made the long drive to the venue with Kate and we were beyond excited to finally be seeing our icon/Mother in real life -- we didn't even care our seats would be horrible and surrounded by conservative republicans complaining about smoke. I would heartbreakingly miss the next two tours despite entering every win-a-ticket contest I could find and trying to be caller whatever on a radio giveaway. In 2012 I got the greatest surprise of my life when my boyfriend left me a note that said to look under the table and taped underneath was an envelope that said, "Strike a pose!" and inside were two tickets to the *MDNA* tour at the Staples center in Los Angeles. A few years later with a more grown-up income I bought tickets to see *Rebel Heart Tour* in Los Angeles and San Jose. I'm a roadie! Then a few years later, I would irresponsibly blow an entire paycheck on one ticket for me to see the *Madame X* theater show third row in the pit! Integrity, motherfuckers!

Madonna's greatest contribution to me as a human is that she taught me what integrity was, being true and not backing down when someone else is threatened by it. She not only showed me gay men, but she also taught me what gay pride was and even let me see two men kiss for the first time. In *Truth or Dare*, when Gabriel crosses the room to Slam, after being dared to kiss him and gets right on top of him for the hottest gay kissing scene ever -- I knew in that moment, oh my God I am totally gay! For some of us Madonna was the only person in our lives that said yes, you can do whatever you want to do, dream the biggest dream, gay straight black, white, be who you are and go for it. I learned that family was more than the people we were born into, that love was something we were all able to give each other.

It has often been said of the LGBTQ community that we are lucky because we get to choose our family, most of the time being cast out of our blood tribe, we get to create bonds with people who are like us. Madonna was the first family I made outside of my immediate circle of dysfunction, she was the ringleader and slowly over time I would build my real family around myself and her. I've been fortunate enough to experience unconditional love through the amazing people that are my friends and now family. To me, it is not the quantity of people that surround you, but the quality of them. As *Truth or Dare* plays on my television each Thanksgiving and people start to arrive and mingle, I think of the younger repressed version of myself and how I wish I could scoop him up and tell him everything is going to be super fabulous someday. I would tell him to hang in there, put black tights on, just put the *Vogue* costume on, put your jacket on and that's your costume, for the night.

Howlin' 4 Hoechlin
@rain20001

One of the reasons I worship @Madonna she helped me realize I can be myself. I shouldn't have to hide being gay. She stood for gay rights from the beginning. On top of that, the donations to AIDS education and prevent as well as visiting children with cancer. #MadonnasHugeHeart

4:38 PM • Apr 30, 2021 • Twitter for iPhone

"I was starstruck by Madonna. She's one of the few remaining superstars. I'm so impressed by her level of discipline towards her career."

– Donna Air

The Crème Caramel Madonna
Artist: Ignacio Miranda
Instagram: @Iggstamatic

MADONNA IN MY LIFE
by Lawrence Stern

It feels as though I have been a fan of Madonna for almost as long as I can remember. Many people have come and gone in my life – fads appear and then vanish – and tastes change over time. Yet, the one constant since my childhood: my love and unwavering support of the true megastar and trailblazer, Madonna.

Ever since the first album was released, I was hooked. I remember being so excited to discover her music and seeing her sing and dance on TV for the first time. I found an album cover square of the self-titled debut (they used to sell these at our local Disc Shop in Washington, DC) and along with photos I clipped from magazines, I decorated my junior high locker with her images. Some of my classmates mocked my enthusiasm for Madonna and her music and claimed she was a flash in the pan. I told them with certainty that she was here to stay. I remember one boy in my school claiming she wouldn't last and that Journey was forever. I guess we proved him wrong.

As time passed my enthusiasm for Madonna and her music only grew. I was lucky to see her very first concert – The Virgin Tour – and my parents were so sweet as they took me and my twin brother to the show and picked us up after (since we were so young). As Madonna's discography continued with such flair and her stardom only skyrocketed – through *Like A Virgin* and *True Blue* – I happily and with great excitement followed every single on the radio, buying so many 45s, and watched every music video release. I was on the floor at the *Who's That*

Girl tour and I eagerly watched all Madonna's films, as she was now becoming a movie star, too.

Blond Ambition remains my favorite concert – by Madonna or any other artist. The spectacle and physicality were astounding. Each number becoming its own intricate set piece. Once again, I was quite close to her and the stage. And this era is also one of the best – including *Like A Prayer* and the *Immaculate Collection*. Madonna truly ruled the world by now – as she had once aspired to do when interviewed by Dick Clark in one of her first TV spots.

I won tickets from the local radio station and attended the DC premiere of the *Dick Tracy* movie, and I even danced with some of her backup dancers from *Blonde Ambition* at the after party. When Madonna made her Broadway debut in *Speed The Plow*, I was there -- front and center. I even went back the next afternoon as I realized where she would exit after the play. I stood in front of her limo outside the theater and when she came out I politely asked if I could take her picture. She smiled at me and nodded -- and I snapped her photo.

Throughout high school and college I was focused on my own academic interests and extracurricular activities – doing tons of shows as an actor during my time at Brown University and shifting my focus to writing for grad school (I got my MFA from UCLA, Summa Cum Laude). Yet anyone who knew me then or now will attest to the fact that I have always remained completely enamored by our Queen of Pop. I was so amazed how Madonna constantly transformed herself and her art, and by the time *Ray of Light* was released I knew she had created yet another masterpiece. A few years later, in 2001, I was set to see her again in concert (over the years, I have been fortunate to watch her live in every single concert tour – only missing *The Girlie Show*) for *Drowned World*. The ticket was for my birthday, September 13, and this performance was so significant and unique, as it came two days after 9/11. She addressed the tragedy and spoke specifically to us about needing to be together and heal, through music, prayer and love. She was crying along with the rest of us and it was a night that was so moving and necessary.

By the time the tickets for the *Confessions on a Dance Floor* tour tickets went on sale, my best friend and I decided we'd drive from Los Angeles to Fresno since we could get first row floor, center catwalk tickets if we went north to see the show. That night when the concert was about to begin, we were in shock at how close we were. But the opening number (*Future Lovers/I Feel Love*) was where something incredible happened. Dressed in a riding outfit and holding a crop/whip, M came down the catwalk as she sang. She stopped when she got to the end of the runway and locked eyes with me. I was beaming and singing along and then she pulled back on the whip and whipped me! I cried out, "Oh my God – Madonna just whipped me!" and Madonna threw her head back and laughed! I knew it would never get any better (though for a few minutes I worried that she might think my friend and I lived in Fresno!).

More films and music (and tours) have come and gone – and each era has its own place in my heart. *Rebel Heart* was a special concert as my friend and I were right in front of the heart portion of the stage and when Madonna did her acoustic numbers we were so moved by her unabashed honest emotion. *Madame X*, the most recent concert, was also terrific, as it was the first time seeing her in such a small intimate venue. I was in the first few rows and couldn't resist going to this show a total of three times! Madonna might not be setting the *Hot 100* on fire these days (though when she did, she achieved all her hits the real and hard way – with sales and airplay, as there was no free streaming like there is now) – yet she remains a true artist and trailblazer.

I eagerly await any new project from her -- in all mediums, and I have tried my best to live my own artistic life as a writer by following one of her mantras: Express Yourself (Don't Repress Yourself). And in current times, which are so tumultuous and terrifying, Madonna continues to provide such wonderful joy and pathos through all her art. It might not be one of her most known recordings, but *Ghosttown* has become my trusted soundtrack for this horrific pandemic. It seems now, more than ever, that Madonna's work transcends time – and her voice still gives me such comfort, entertainment, and inspiration.

Patty Bourrée
@PattyBourree

Madonna came to me in a dream last night and told me im a bottom.

8:03 AM • May 31, 2021 • Twitter for iPhone

"You can think what you like of Madonna - about her political choices and her PR - but you have to respect her courage not to let the critics stop her exploring her potential."

– Natalie Dormer

Queen of Pop
Artist: Maria Antoinette van Schooten-Krzeminski
Instagram: @maria_krzeminksa

A GIRL WHO LOVED TO DANCE
by LeeAnn Tooker

Growing up I wanted to be a dancer. I had a lot of natural ability but was very aware that "real" dancers had started ballet training at an early age. I had definitely started dancing at an early age, but expensive dance lessons were not likely a priority for my stressed-out single mother. So the dancing went on in my room, the garage, and sometimes an empty classroom to which my friends and I had snuck away. I became accustomed to figuring out how to do things for myself and by age 11, I was a pretty determined kid. I wasn't shy, or quiet, or often supervised. And so, though I don't remember the details, I found a way to get ballet classes paid for and I walked or took the bus after school to get there. At just 4'3" tall, I carried a large black dance bag that was nearly half my body size. Sometimes I also carried with me a small backpack or other bag. Showing up to the prestigious Houston Ballet Academy, sweaty, disheveled, and dragging around big bags was a stark contrast to the little girls being dropped off from air-conditioned sedans with perfect ballet buns, flawless dancewear, and involved parents. I never did master the bun. Or any of it really.

    I performed well in dance class and felt secure there, but outside of class I felt I was seen as different when in the lobby or dressing room of the academy. It was the same 'different' that I felt when I had attended an expensive private school up until just the year prior. While I did have friends at private school, the great differences in our lives were blatant and I often felt inferior - financially, family relationship wise, or both. Now, at the ballet academy, I was again being viewed as different but was handling it better this time around. I had left the private school. I was now attending a public school and I liked it there. More importantly though, by now I had come to know about the coolest, most badass dancer and performer to ever live, my soulmate – Madonna!

At that time, if someone were to have referred to me as a Madonna fan, I would've felt the need to explain that I wasn't just a "fan". A fan was some basic girl who thought Madonna was cool. That wasn't me. Madonna and I had a special connection. Madonna understood my desire to be a dancer. Madonna had to struggle. Madonna didn't come from money. Madonna was different, but amazing. And I was amazing too, even if no one realized it yet but me! Further, Madonna not only didn't care if people thought she was different - she *wanted* to be different. I remember reading that when Madonna studied dance, she held her leotards together with safety pins and I loved this rebellion against tradition! I went from just being okay that I was seen as different in these environments, to fully embracing it. I should note that even now, as a woman in her 40's, I hesitate to share about my connection with Madonna lest someone reading this assume that their love for her is in any way comparable to mine. You have to understand, what Madonna and I have is *special*.

The kids in my public middle school understood. No one was as 'Madonna' as I was in middle school. I often went to school dressed in a Madonna vibe. I danced for kids in the neighborhood, marching out to the corner with my jam box, Madonna's *Borderline* blaring, and danced until a small group of kids on my block had gathered around watching. And because many of my friends lived in an affluent neighborhood and I came from a suburb across town, pulling off a Desperately-Seeking-Susan-esque, street-smart persona was not difficult. In addition to feeling cool like Madonna, this street-smart confidence afforded me some internal strength, something quite helpful to me growing up in a volatile home environment. While I was typically always one of the smallest kids in my grade, I never felt so.

Near the end of the school year in 1985, Madonna's first concert tour would be in my city just a couple of days before my birthday. Concert tickets, to a concert that would also require transportation to said concert, were another item definitely not on my mother's priority list. As such, I'm certain that I spent zero time fantasizing about going to Madonna's *Like a Virgin* tour. It wasn't going to happen and to dream of such a thing would simply be too painful. You can imagine my surprise and elation when a girl in my class whom I knew, but not all that well, offered me both a ticket and a ride to the Madonna concert. Her parents were treating her and like ten of her friends to this night out!

It was my very first concert experience and the only one that would ever mean so much. Sitting amongst ten or so of my middle school classmates, as Madonna took the stage, I was overcome with emotion. I started crying at the realization that I was breathing the same air as Madonna! Yes, our seats were very high up and it was a huge stadium, but it was enclosed so we were sharing air as far as I was concerned. My friends, understanding that this was an amazing moment for me, were attentive and sweet as I composed myself. I soon abandoned the confinement of the seats, choosing to dance the entire concert in an open area behind our seating. I was super proud when afterwards, as concert-goers walked down the cement ramps to exit, I overheard several adult strangers make comments like, "Hey, that's the girl that was dancing all night!" and "There's that little Madonna!" Even they saw that what Madonna and I have is special.

Madonna is woven through so many of my memories. In a time without social media or the internet, I fed my Madonna cravings by collecting any image of Madonna that I came across. My bedroom walls were covered with magazine and newspaper photos as small as a square inch to posters as large as 5' x 7'. It was impressive. A school friend and I recreated the *Material Girl* video on her family Handycam. Naturally, I had the role of Madonna and she and her sister were dressed in makeshift tuxedos beside me. I remember thinking we really nailed it, and then years later, being mortified when while watching videos with her grandparents, she stumbled upon the VHS tape of 12-year-old me writhing on a couch. That said, I still would not change this memory for anything.

I choreographed dances with a friend in her backyard to the *True Blue* album and danced my way into the Performing Arts High School. I memorized all the choreography for the *Open Your Heart* music video and would often perform it only partially-clothed in our living room, much to my brother's dismay. To this day, if given enough alcohol, I will perform that same choreography when the song is played, regardless of where we happen to be. I went to the *Who's That Girl* World Tour and the *Blonde Ambition* World Tour, both instances in which a friend covered my ticket. Looking back, I am so grateful for these generous friends! I had my first (and only) one-night stand with a guy after several drinks and some amazing club dancing to *Justify My Love*. Fortunately, I wasn't murdered and at least the guy could dance pretty well.

As any true Madonna fan, I awaited with bated breath the arrival of Madonna's much talked about *Sex* book. Living in conservative Texas meant that I also had to navigate many rumors about the book's contents before its release. My journal entries from that time hysterically show me wrestling with having been told that the book had both pictures of Madonna "fucking a dog" and "fucking her sister" (both untrue). To quote the diary writings of my younger self, "If these pictures are, in fact, in the book, then Madonna is not considering her responsibility in the role of Superstar". Hilarious. Also, the dog photo was one of my favorites.

Of course, there were numerous Madonna-inspired DIY photo shoots throughout the years. I recently came across a thumbnail image on a contact sheet from one of those shoots. My friend and I had decided to take some sexy photos and I specifically wanted to try to recreate the black and white Madonna *Justify My Love* image. The iconic photo shows Madonna wearing a black leather cap and leather vest, arms crossed in front of her chest with attitude and a cigarette dangling from her pouty mouth. In the 90s, we didn't have cell phone cameras, filters, or photo apps so this photo project was quite an undertaking. We bought black and white film - film that we understood would later have to be developed (and seen) by some guy at Walgreens. We pressed on. We collected props and sexy clothing items throughout the week. I dodged giving my boyfriend any specifics about the project and banned him from being in the apartment on the day. On the morning of the shoot, we hung a white bed sheet across the wall, opened up all the blinds, and brought in every lamp and light source from the entire apartment into one room. We played Madonna music and took turns being the model. Janet Jackson's *Janet* album was out at this time and one of the promotional photos showed a topless Janet in a pair of jeans with someone reaching around from behind her to hold her breasts. In my head, I must've morphed

Janet's promo image with that of Madonna's *Justify My Love* image because the guy at Walgreens developed photos of me wearing a black leather cap, arms crossed in front of my bare chest, each hand clutching a boob (with attitude) and a cigarette dangling from my mouth.

Somewhere in my early 20's, I got a tattoo to compliment my belly ring and then later that same evening, while lying in bed staring up at a framed poster of Madonna in a black vinyl bikini with a chain (ala *Human Nature*), I completely freaked out because I realized that Madonna did not have any permanent markings on her body and I had just tattooed a very permanent black tribal art sun on my stomach. I spent the bulk of the next day researching tattoo removal, which was no small feat back then, sans internet. I ended up keeping the tattoo and grew to love it until my stomach also grew, but that's another story.

I had a particularly vivid dream once about Madonna that I can still see so clearly in my mind. We were best friends (duh) and living together in a huge house. We each had a bedroom on opposite ends of the home. My bedroom had a skylight in the ceiling above my bed and in the dream, I was waking up to the day. As I stared at the skylight, I started thinking about the party that Madonna and I were throwing that night. I suppose thinking about all the details for our extravagant party must've stressed me out and snapped me awake because then I found myself in my real bed and my real life. It was gut-wrenching! You know when you were younger and had a dream that all your teeth fell out and then when you woke up and realized it was just a dream, and you were so grateful? Well, this was the opposite of that.

Even as my personal dreams morphed through the years from dancer to dancer/singer, to actor, to stand-up comedian, my love for Madonna has never wavered. Each of her transformations only made me love her more and showed me that people change and evolve. You shouldn't always be the same thing. This perspective really allowed me to explore different sides of myself, goth-phase and all.

Through all of my personal growth and life moments, there has always been an accompanying Madonna soundtrack. I am grateful that this continues to be true as she just keeps creating. Madonna has been such an inspiration to me. She is a woman with such strength, confidence, courage, sexuality, love, and willingness to explore. A woman who doesn't care about your rules. A woman who knows her worth and invites you to know yours. A woman who accomplished much, learned much and still continues to do so. A woman who started as a girl who loved to dance. Like me.

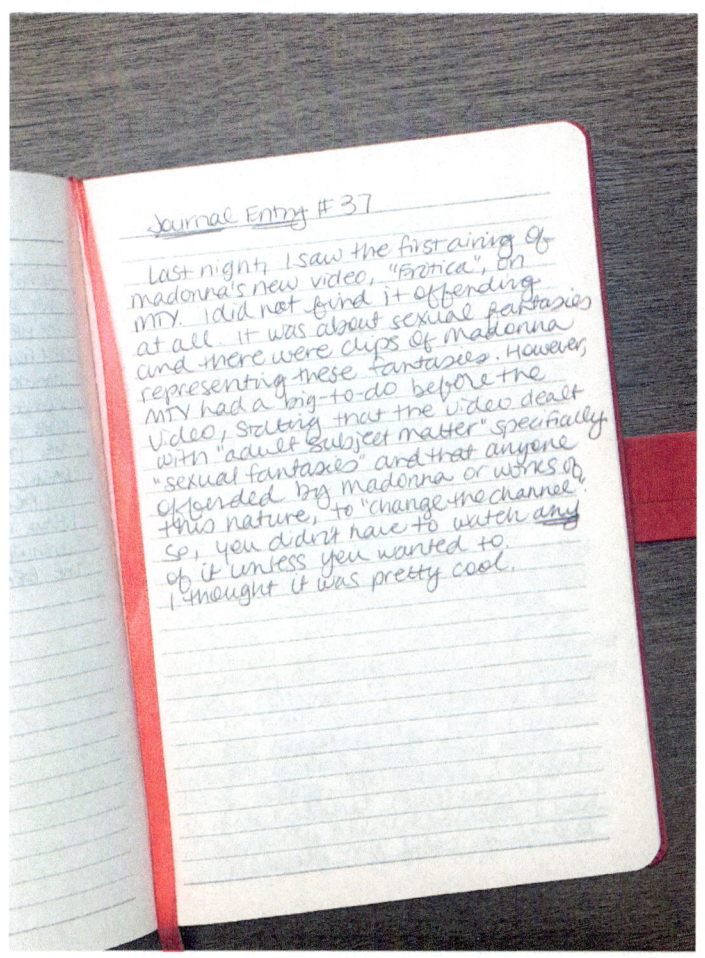

Journal Entry #37

Last night I saw the first airing of Madonna's new video, "Erotica", on MTV. I did not find it offending at all. It was about sexual fantasies. However, MTV had a big to-do before the video, stating that the video dealt with "adult subject matter" specifically "sexual fantasies" and that anyone offended by Madonna or works of this nature, [should] "change the channel". So, you didn't have to watch any of it unless you wanted to. I thought it was pretty cool.

LeeAnn's Journal (1992)

"Popular culture still reeks of her influence"

– Barbara Ellen

Tears of a Clown - Art Basel 2016
Artist: Gerardo Alvino
Instagram: @_gerardo_alvino_

MY MADONNA STORY
by Saima Huq

Madonna was 1985 personified. She showed up from Detroit with a beauty mark and a gap in her teeth, accepting jewelry while rocking a pink satin evening gown in an ironic homage to Marilyn Monroe in 1953's *Gentlemen Prefer Blondes*. Here she was saying she wanted all the nice things in life too -- and you know what? She could have them without anyone's say-so because she fucking earned it.

She showed us that we could fucking earn it. It's not the hair color or skin color you were born to. Why be a princess when you can be a Rockstar? Rock stars earn it and Madonna was pure rock star. This was powerful stuff for every girl in the 1980s, but particularly those who dared to be non-white in a white-centered world. Madonna showed us she was who she was because she felt like it, not because society gave her permission to be.

Madonna was *inclusive*. She belonged to herself and showed you that you could do the same. Stop living by the script that you have to be popular in high school and be a cheerleader, or be mean to be "funny". Shed everyone's opinions that make you miserable. What do their boring asses know? Fast forward 30 years and they will have back tats and a realtor's license in the town they never left, and Madonna will be Madonna several times over, all around the world.

She dressed up with a lacy bow in her bouncy hair, fingerless gloves and tutus. She was as New York trash and vaudeville as the store on Saint Mark's Place bearing the same name. I watched her as Breathless Mahoney in *Dick Tracy* on my 17th birthday in a now-closed theatre in a now-closed mall. She vogued in black and white in 1990 and I later danced those moves in lavender at a same-sex wedding in New York with the LGBTQ club kids who were also cast out in high school. We bonded with each other. Madonna created that bond for us, and the beat goes on over 30 years later for all of us.

Thank you, Madonna!

Joshua
@Joshua95366493

If you are feeling down or negative about yourself, just think of our Queen and be flawless because you are beautiful inside and out no matter what anyone says!! #madonnafamily #madonna

8:00 AM • Dec 9, 2021 • Twitter for Android

"All of the artists that I've worked with have an incredible work ethic. And Madonna has the best work ethic of them all. I've learned a lot from being around her."

– Paul Oakenfold

Madonna, watercolor portrait
Artist: Matías Alejandro Cabrera
Instagram: @matiatzukun

MY MADONNA
by Patricia White

    I still own the last stapled issue of Playboy magazine. Madonna was on the cover and she embodied coy seduction and mystery. I saw someone I wanted to be -- smart, talented, ambitious and famous. Some of my most favorite memories of Madonna come over me in a dream-like wave.

    I was sixteen and was headed out to school. I put on lace stockings and a bustier under my school clothes. I packed a mini-skirt and heels in my backpack so my siblings or parents wouldn't notice. I teased and sprayed my hair extra high that day, and I wrapped a lace headband and tied it on the side - allowing the extra ribbon to cascade into the field of hair sprayed stiffness. I added rubber bangles to both wrists and packed my lipstick in my purse - and off to school I went.

    The day went by quickly enough and I told nobody, not even my friends, what I was up to. As soon as the dismissal bell rang I drove to the Dobbs Ferry train station and boarded Metro North to Grand Central. My heart was pounding. I had never scalped a ticket before. I had eighty bucks on me and just enough change to take the train back home.

    I had no idea where I was going so I asked and soon found myself on the steps outside Madison Square Garden. Now in full Madonna gear, I fearlessly walked up to the scalper and pretended I knew him. I told him to give me a hug as I slipped the $75 cash into his hand in exchange for the ticket.

There she was in all her glory - my hero - Madonna. She rolled on the stage and sang with the same confidence and seduction that was in each photo. She was a professional all the way. She knew her brand and she was in complete control. She worked hard. She loved hard. She hurt hard. And I loved her for all of it.

Another time I was approaching the Yonkers toll booth on NYS Thruway when one of her songs became Number 1 on Top 40. I remember cheering for her, like it had been me who achieved the victory. I remember being truly happy for her. We had succeeded, for she was a part of me.

I saw a more vulnerable side of Madonna when she held Lourdes, who was at the time an infant. She asked her baby, "Do you have something important to say?" I saw her love. I finally saw Madonna Louise Ciccone from Michigan. Catholic. Italian. A one-of-a-kind person who doesn't take shit from anybody had evolved into a loving mother.

And she still rocks it.

Tommy Natoli
@TommyNatoli

Have to watch Madonna concert on tiny laptop screen. Furious gay guy here. Furious.

7:58 PM • Jun 23, 2013 • Twitter Web Client

"She was down-to-earth Madonna... She's just brutally honest about a lot of stuff: 'I'm doing this, I'm not going to sing that.' She's very matter-of-fact but still very fun and loving and into her craft."

– Timbaland

F(OR)EVER
Artist: Matthew Rettenmund
Instagram: @encyclopediamadonnica

AND YOU CAN DANCE, FOR INSPIRATION…
by Lisa Gopman

As a chubby Jewish girl in the Christian suburbs of Ohio, I knew deep in my heart that not only did I not belong, but rebellion was in my soul. The vanilla attitudes of my uber uptight classmates and parents and their music were an ongoing struggle, and Madonna was my constant spiritual guide reminding me to keep *off* the beaten path. She always seemed to pop up at the perfect moment, as if to tell me that I was in the right place being just as weird as I was supposed to be, and possibly even more importantly -- to just dance. Madonna Dance Parties are this Jewish girl's burning bush.

For as long as I can remember my heart has wanted a dance party. In fact, in first grade my boyfriend Jon Hart and I won Best Dancers when we danced to *Beat It* at the school assembly. Spoiler alert, we were pretty amazing. But when I finally talked my mom into splurging on dance classes, ballet was the most appropriate dance form for me because "slutty girls" took jazz and even sluttier girls took *gasp*, clogging. #Ohio. I quit ballet after the first recital because learning all the positions was so tedious and all I wanted to do was jump and twirl. And Lord, those white leotards were not flattering on my already curvy 8-year-old thighs. Sadly, my professional dancing career never went any further however as recently as January 2020 I was involved in a very heated birthday dance-off with a Tony nominee in NYC, but let's stay focused on Madonna (clearly I've got hundreds of pivotal dance party moments to distract us).

The first time I got grounded for dancing to Madonna was for playing after school in 3rd grade with my equally repressed Catholic across-the-street-neighbor. Her cousin had gotten her the *Like a Virgin* cassette tape for her birthday. Now *this* was some music I could dance to! We'd blast her boom box while quietly slipping off our tops and dancing in our training bras. Until the day her mom came up with some surprise snacks and blew a Catholic gasket! That was the end of our mutual dancing and sadly the end of my friendship with that neighbor. Though it would not be the end of me dancing provocatively in what was basically my underwear (because duh, I lived through the 90's).

Onto Ms. Bragan, my 4th grade language arts teacher with a Southern drawl. She seemed conservative but had a mischievous sparkle in her eye that made me wonder even at age 9 what she was getting into after school. She was one of my favorite teachers and wanted us to really appreciate language so she gave us the assignment to pair up and perform a lip sync of our favorite song. My best friend Tami and I looked at each other and we knew without pause that *Material Girl* would have to be our song! We also knew choosing a Madonna piece wouldn't mean just singing, so we spent days in my newly finished Ohio basement, practicing our brilliant choreography. Some highlights of the performance included doing The Robot during the male robotic voice, and for the lyric "Only boys who save their pennies make my rainy day," we both revealed and then threw out our bags of pennies. Genius. I don't know how Madonna hasn't hired me to choreograph one of her tours but perhaps she's reading this right now and thinking she must! Our lip sync was quite successful. Tami and I, however, had a silly classic high school falling out -- but when we did reconnect years later, one of the first things we reminisced over was that magical lip sync. It was literally our favorite friendship memory.

Madonna continued to color my extremely bland suburban existence. While I tried not to be sheltered in Ohio, I couldn't help but be in the dark on some topics -- particularly the gay scene at the time. Ironic, considering it would become such an important part of my life and identity down the yellow brick road. However, born and raised in Cincinnati, Ohio, I had literally *zero* gaydar. Enter Todd. Aww. Sweet, drop dead gorgeous, Puerto Rican Todd. He was 25 and the hottest step aerobics instructor at my gym. Because yes, in my current struggle to fit in I'd become weirdly obsessed with the gym. In retrospect, he probably shouldn't have been taking a 17-year-old to Homecoming. I couldn't believe it when my dad said it was okay. Why did no one stop it? Because hello, he was so gay! He was the perfect date. He made me feel like a princess. However, mid-dance I left at the worst possible moment to go pee. Lisa, how could you leave when *Vogue* came on?! As I hustled back to the dance floor I noticed a huge circle around one person. Everyone was screaming and cheering. Who could this be? Probably Darci Abraham's date, ugh. I wish I was popular like her. But as I got closer I realized it was Todd -- my date! -- and the entire high school was in a circle around him as he Vogue-d his hot little ass off. I thought "wow, I'm the luckiest girl here. Look how everyone is looking at him and then me." I was thinking this is probably my future husband, but couldn't help but notice he wasn't signaling me to join him as he continued to vogue by himself in the spotlight. After the dance he got me into a real life 21 and up bar and we got wasted (it was my first time doing both of those things, but clearly not the last)– and somehow, I only got grounded for a week. That was one of the best nights of my entire high school life, and the beginning of my beautiful connection and now full-on obsession with the gay community. Madonna had brought me to my people.

    I would be so lost in life without my gay besties. In fact, I would turn out to be quite the "hag." I know the kids today prefer "fruit fly" or "best gal," but I'm old school, I'm a *hag*! In 1995 I had finally made it out of Ohio and I was definitely struggling to figure out who I was and was desperately seeking my tribe. That first week of college in LA I realized just how sheltered I'd been when my new roommates literally held me down and plucked my eyebrows. I had no idea you were supposed to pluck your eyebrows! By 1998 I was a theatre major who was wild and dating everyone but spent most of my time hanging out with tons of gay friends. When I had my epiphany I was at a super fun house party. I was definitely very drunk and on the dance floor with one of my gay besties, Michael. I had never seen so many drop-dead gorgeous guys and so many curvy girls. Hmmm. That's interesting. I hadn't really noticed that fetish before. I looked around. "Wow. I kind of like this scene... No skinny bitches allowed, and so many hot guys to choose from!" And then it happened. *Ray of Light* came on -- and for lack of a better phrase, every single dude at the party just began to "gay out" (as we called it in 1998). As Madonna so brilliantly said herself, "Music can be such a revelation" because at that moment, I went to grind into Michael, and a giant rainbow lightbulb went off in my brain: "Holy Shit. Every guy here is looking at each other. Omg. Every single guy here is gay!" That was the magical moment the Queen of Pop enlightened me to the fact that I was a hag -- and I've embraced and loved the shit out of it since.

I could barely contain my excitement when in 2008 one of my best gay friends told me that he could get us Madonna tickets for a show at Dodger Stadium. This is one of my longest gay besties and he also happens to be from Michigan, so he's die-hard Madonna, and we are *so* Midwest. In fact, we are arguably more Midwest when we are together. So, to be honest, there were a few issues with our plan. The most challenging being that my friend, we'll call him John, had to work. But we formulated a plan and discussed that even if we were late, it's *Madonna!* And you only live once. And we could not believe that we hadn't seen her yet. It was criminal. We knew we were just going to die if we didn't see her sing one song and it'd be worth all of our money. It was going to be all our Madonna dance party dreams come true!

The day finally came and sure enough, John had to work late. Ugh. I was getting stressed but obviously was also stressing about my outfit. I decided I needed to be 80's vibe cute. John finally picked me up and there was no way we weren't going to be late. As we headed towards Dodger Stadium it happened -- traffic came to a complete standstill. *Fuck.* "How is this even possible? The show starts in like a half hour and we aren't even close!" We sat in traffic for an hour and a half. We legit didn't know what to do. Should we give up? Should we turn around? We technically hadn't picked up our tickets yet so thought maybe we could get our money back... But then we returned to our senses and rallied. "This is Madonna! We have to." We finally got there and raced to our seats. We were completely sober which was definitely not our original plan at all. But there she was. She looked amazing and was hilarious and sassy as fuck -- just like we wanted her to be. Someone in the front was holding up a sign requesting *Dress You Up* and she's like, "Really? Are you sure? That's seriously not my best song and I don't even know if I remember the words." We were laughing with glee as she sang a few verses and then was quickly over it. After killing a few classics, Justin Timberlake came out and they sang *4 Minutes* which I was obsessed with at the time and we were both like – "Omg, this is the hottest moment of our lives and the 10-hour drive was all worth it!" And it was. Madonna put on one hell of a show. I would have been so mad at myself if I had missed having that ultimate Madonna dance party celebration with my longtime gay bestie who means the world to me!

No matter what has been going on in my life, Madonna has been giving me all the moments. The Material Girl has been taking us all on her life journey and her music has always provided the quintessential soundtrack to mine. Especially for me and my beloved gay friends. And for that I will be eternally grateful. Madonna has always given my life more meaning. The feeling I get when a Madonna song starts playing and I lock eyes with my gay friends is a love and sense of belonging that I deeply cherish.

Thank you, Madonna. I feel like you have unlocked this huge, magical wonderland into our souls. Be it clubbing with my bestie Stevie B in Hollywood in the early aughts, or the late nineties when I studied abroad in Madrid and would somehow consistently find myself stumbling through the streets inappropriately screaming *La Isla Bonita* with an empty porron of Sangria, or in the eighties dancing with Mary Beth in my training bra; Madonna was with me -- letting me know we all go through those phases of searching, we all feel lost, and none of us should settle for staying somewhere we don't feel like we belong, because in the end we will always find our people. Madonna continually reminded me that if you just listen… music brings the people together. And most importantly, no matter where we are in life, we really all should be dancing!

Juanito
@JUANITOMG

#MadonnaFanProblems Taking a Bio class and everytime the word 'DNA' comes up you read it as MDNA.

11:03 PM • Mar 20, 2013 • Twitter Web Client

"Do I envy Madonna's body? Yes. Do I thank God that she has it? Yes! If you're fifty-something and you look like Madonna, and you put a lifetime's work in the way you look, then flash it to the world!"

– Salma Hayek

Eyes the Color of Water
Artist: H. Louis Tooker

BORDERLINE
by Faye Rapoport DesPres

In 1984 I spent five months teaching fitness and aerobics at a Jack LaLanne health club in Rockland County, New York. The club was located in a strip mall across the Hudson River and a half hour north of New York City. I'd just finished college, and I was taking a semester off before heading to graduate school.

Aerobics classes were gaining in popularity at the time; Jane Fonda had released the first of her popular workout tapes in 1982. I was a gymnast in high school and a swimming instructor and lifeguard during summer vacations from college, so a job at a gym seemed like a good way to make some money.

Training for the job involved spending a week at a Jack LaLanne headquarters with a small group of strangers dressed in sweat suits and sneakers. One weightlifter with ripped muscles smoked cigarettes during our breaks. We practiced proper techniques for using the Nautilus machines that were popular at the time and sweated through aerobics classes to learn the moves we would teach. At the end of the week, the management team handed out pre-mixed cassette tapes we were instructed to use for our classes.

Thirty-six years later, I still have Cassette #8, with the number written in black marker on one side. For years after I'd moved on from the job, it remained in a tape deck in the attic at my parents' house, where I could turn it on whenever I felt like giving myself a class.

At the health club, #8 was my go-to music for class. The steady drone of Tina Turner's *What's Love Got to Do With It* got everyone reaching their arms towards the ceiling during the warmup. Miquel Brown's disco-thumping *He's a Saint He's a Sinner* was perfect for some grapevines traveling back and forth across the room. We were cooking by the time the club mix of *High Energy* by Evelyn Thomas blared through the speakers. To this day, Prince's *When Doves Cry* makes me want to drop to the floor and do crunches. But what has stayed with me most about that claustrophobic room, with its ceiling-to-floor mirrors, padded floor, and stay-at-home moms filing in every hour, was doing low-impact cardio to Madonna's *Borderline*.

Madonna, twenty-six then, had released her debut album the previous year. The record featured addictive tinsel beats and brash vocals, and its catchy tunes were in heavy rotation on the radio. The new "Queen of Pop" pranced with brazen confidence through MTV videos, her teased hair wrapped in oversized bows, her lips painted red, her ears dripping with dangly earrings while her arms were wrapped in thick bracelets, her body adorned with anything from denim to black leather or flirty lace. Chains laden with oversized crosses circled her neck or waist. Madonna was a crafted combination of rebellious punk and pop; she skirted the line between the outcast and the mainstream, using the very machine she raged against to launch her music career.

Teen girls euphorically pounced on their new icon. They dressed like her when attending her concerts and copied her loose-limbed, choreographed dance moves. They explored the concept of female empowerment as Madonna turned societal expectations about women inside out, just as she wore brassieres as blouses. She dared to be a woman unapologetically driven by her sexuality, instead of apologizing for it. She tossed caution and female modesty to the wind, claiming the right to both feel and be treated like a virgin while declaring proudly that she had zero interest in being one.

Meanwhile, in Rockland County, I headed to a health club named for a man every day wearing a T-shirt with the gym's logo, running shorts worn over dark blue tights, ankle socks, and white Reebok sneakers. I surreptitiously watched Tina, a pretty, popular aerobics instructor with carefully styled light brown hair, as she smiled without irony and chatted easily with the members. She was taller and had more confidence than me, and her hips were slimmer than mine. At five-foot-one I was insecure about my muscular frame. Unlike long-limbed Jane Fonda or the public Madonna, I had never felt comfortable in my own skin.

In retrospect, the truth was I'd never had Madonna's guts. A relatively shy good girl who was born in New York City but had been raised further north in farm country, I'd brought a raccoon-shaped pillow and a cat cartoon comforter to my college dorm at the start of my freshman year. I sang folk songs while strumming an acoustic guitar. Throughout high school and college I had the dubious reputation of being "nice."

Rebellion for me meant wearing a Grateful Dead T-shirt, sewing a "Friend of Animals" patch on my torn Levi jeans, and sporting a brown leather Australian Stetson borrowed from my father. I woke up to fashion while studying English and Theatre Arts in London during my junior year, but just barely. For the most part, to me, King's Road was a tourist attraction.

Maybe that's why I couldn't stop watching Madonna's videos. While I was counting members' reps on the leg press or dip machines and encouraging suburban women to feel the burn, Madonna was blowing the lid off conventional American life. She shoved her untamed attitude and gyrating body in our faces, and a part of me couldn't turn away.

It would be years before I'd understand what it all meant — a full decade before, at the age of 32, I'd walk out of a seven-month marriage because I'd realized I had no idea who I really was. But in 1984, I was an aerobics instructor in a warehouse-shaped strip mall doing donkey kicks and fire hydrants to Madonna's *Borderline*. Looking back, I can't help but wonder if that's when the seed to my rebellion was planted. The following year, Madonna played a drifter in the movie *Desperately Seeking Susan*, the antithesis of Rosanna Arquette's bored housewife. Her character was also the antithesis of who I was then, but not of the woman waiting patiently inside me for her chance to bloom.

A few months after *Desperately Seeking Susan* hit cinema screens, Madonna performed on the American stage at *Live Aid*. I remember thinking that the decision to include her was strange. The likes of David Bowie, Paul McCartney, Queen, and U2 were on the list of performers at Wembley in London. In the States, we had Bob Dylan, Tom Petty, and Black Sabbath. What was Madonna, a relative newcomer, doing on that stage? Dressed in flowery pants and a pale hip-length jacket of lime green, a trademark cross hanging from her neck, Madonna opened with the upbeat song *Holiday*. Was she seeing the event as a party or celebration, not an effort to raise money for famine victims in Ethiopia? The crowd on TV appeared bemused at first, the concert-goers unsure whether or not to clap along. But they did.

I recently watched Madonna's *Live Aid* performance again, and I see it so differently now. What confidence a twenty-seven-year-old woman must have had to take that stage on that day. She'd faced a scandal a few weeks earlier when *Playboy* and *Penthouse* published nude photos of her taken before she became famous (seven years later, she'd turn that scandal on its head, like everything else, by releasing her own nude photos in a book titled *Sex*). Bette Midler introduced Madonna at *Live Aid*, telling the massive crowd that she was "thrilled" to introduce "a woman who pulled herself up by her bra straps and has been known to let them down occasionally."

Madonna got out there and boldly sang and danced. Writing in *Billboard* years later, Joe Lynch called the performance "one of the most exuberant live performances of her entire career." Watching it now, I wonder if Madonna was saying -- *I'm here. I'm not going anywhere. Deal with it*.

How easy it was then — and still is today — to downplay the determination and drive of a successful woman, especially one who doesn't apologize for who she is. How quickly even I defaulted to the idea that she didn't belong. In truth, it was me who I believed didn't belong. After all, instead of moving into the city to audition for plays, I had stuck myself in the middle of nowhere, doing sit-ups in counts of eight at Jack LaLanne.

A decade later, I returned to that town in Rockland County. But this time, instead of aerobics, I studied and taught martial arts. I earned my black belt, and then my second and third degrees. My outfit was the same black gi the men wore, and my feet were as bare during training as theirs. In fact, over the years since I peeled off blue tights for the last time, I've been through quite a few transitions. I dated a number of men, packed up my belongings and moved to Colorado, returned to the east coast, and left my last office job. For many years I watched friends marry and have children while I remained alone. At times I was desperately lonely, and I questioned my choices. But I was finding my own way to be free.

From what I've read, Madonna has changed a lot, too. She's still recording and performing, but she's a mother of six now with two divorces in her own rear-view mirror. I don't know her personally, and I have no idea how she feels about her life now. But my guess is she's still giving whatever she does all she can. With the shadow of her '80s self still dancing in chains in the corner of my eye, so am I.

Uncle Heather
@heatherturman

Happy Birthday to the only Baby Boomer who actually improved upon the world, @madonna

11:28 AM • Aug 16, 2021 • Twitter for iPhone

"Her work is so vast -- there's a reference for any situation."

— SOPHIE

True Blue
Artist: H. Louis Tooker

MADONNA MOMENTS
by Nick Musmecci

Madonna has an uncanny way of hitting me on multiple levels. As an icon I am awestruck at her success and her unparalleled dedication to innovation and reinvention. As a storyteller I admire her willingness to push the envelope and bare it all in her lyrics. As an entertainer I can't appreciate enough the way she leaves it all out on any stage she steps on. Most importantly though, I appreciate the way her music and movies have brought me closer together with people in my life and provided a soundtrack to some of the best times I've had. As I look back, I realize my life is full of Madonna moments.

My early exposure to Madonna came in the form of one of my favorite movies as a kid. That would be *A League of Their Own*. Baseball was my first love as a child and I am pretty sure I watched every baseball movie that came out between 1986 and 2000. While Madonna was far from the main focus of the movie, she definitely made an indelible mark on me and I have to admit that between her role in *Dick Tracy* and her scene stealing performance as "All the Way Mae," twelve-year-old me had a crush on Madonna. I will always remember my Grandma June, who recently passed away and was an accomplished softball player, the first time we watched the movie saying, "You can't slide in that!" in near perfect unison with Madonna when the girls were shown their less-than-practical uniforms.

Fast forward a decade, my 20-year-old-self went and fell in love. As is the case in such complicated matters things didn't go as planned. Both of us were moving around a lot and many goodbyes had to be said.

During one of those goodbyes my ex made me a mixtape and the last song was *Take A Bow* off of Madonna's *Bedtime Stories* album. So heartbroken was twenty-year-old me sitting in the Greyhound station listening to this tape all sad and depressed and this song just absolutely blew me away. I am sure I had heard it before but at that moment that song was just perfection. I didn't keep the tape and I kind of forgot about the song for a few years — but fate was going to reintroduce me to it, and a whole lot more Madonna, a few years down the line.

In 2007 I was working at a restaurant at the famous Hollywood and Highland complex in Hollywood, California. I made friends with a new hire named Heather (she's one of the awesome gals who organized this sweet anthology), and she worships Madonna. Heather and I were both hosts and as we were getting to know each other, music came up and she started talking about Madonna with the same fervor I talked about Garth Brooks, Bruce Springsteen, Tom Petty and the rest of my heroes. My curiosity was piqued and so I downloaded some Madonna on the old iPod.

My first listen to *The Immaculate Collection* turned a fifteen-minute walk home into an hour-long stroll through Hollywood that had me dancing (couldn't have been pretty), singing along (probably sounded fine but still strange) and just thoroughly enjoying this intricate tapestry of pop excellence. It's still in heavy rotation on my playlists to this day, along with a ton of other Madonna songs. I became a true Madonna fan that day. From the opening of *Borderline* to the outro of *Rescue Me*, I was hooked. The sweetness of *Cherish* still makes me smile and the sexiness of *Crazy for You* still makes me swoon. *Vogue* and *Get Into the Groove* are staples on my "Get Up" playlist. It's an all time, desert island record for me.

After that first listen to *Immaculate*, I rediscovered *Take a Bow* and the entire *Bedtime Stories* record as well as *Ray of Light*, *Music* and *American Life*. The juxtaposition of those records really amazed me and helped me solve a problem that was haunting my own music. As a musician I was struggling a lot with what my "sound" was supposed to be. I felt like I needed to define myself and find a genre that fit my "brand." After listening to those three Madonna records I realized that it was much more important to embrace what was coming out of you as an artist and work with it, than trying to make something based on some preconceived notion of what you are "supposed" to sound like. I will forever be grateful to the High Priestess of Pop for helping me feel free to just make my music and not worry about it fitting into some metaphorical box.

That time period in my late twenties is chock full of Madonna moments. Doing a double feature of *Swept Away* and *The Next Best Thing*, both of which I thoroughly enjoyed. Getting hammered and then waiting in line with Heather to buy *Hard Candy* the night it came out was a total blast… I might have accidentally shoplifted a fedora from Virgin Megastore that night… oops. Watching *Truth or Dare* and *I'm Going to Tell You a Secret* offered so much insight into the ups and downs of success and made the music that much more meaningful. Such good times!

I am also lucky to be married to a Madonna fan and she provided me with one of my favorite Madonna moments of all time. The weekend we met she was the event coordinator for my brother's wedding. It was a destination wedding and it was pretty chaotic. As soon as she stepped out of the rental car in her blue flip-flops, I was enamored with her. We started flirting immediately and I became her de facto number two for the weekend. Cut to the day of the wedding and the dance floor arrived and was assembled. She walked up and said that we needed to test the dance floor out. She walked over to the portable speaker and plugged in her iPod and the unmistakable intro of *Get Into the Groove* started playing. She cranked it up and everyone working stopped what they were doing and hit the floor for an impromptu dance party. After the song was over, I told my brother that I was falling for the wedding coordinator – and as of this writing, that coordinator and I just celebrated our own six-year wedding anniversary. I will always give Madonna credit for helping me find the love of my life.

So whether she's helping me find a girl or helping me get over one, inspiring me artistically, keeping me company on long walks home, or just plain being who she is and entertaining the hell out of me – I am beyond grateful to Madonna for the countless moments she has helped create. Here's to many more Madonna moments!

Alan Bennett Ilagan
@alanilagan

The only David Letterman shows I ever watched were the ones with @Madonna. Duh.

1:57 PM • Apr 3, 2014 • Twitter Web Client

"I admire Madonna because she always did whatever she felt like doing. She went through some controversial periods when people rejected her, but she kept on reinventing herself."

– Shakira

Bondage Blue Eyes
Artist: Amber Gignac
Website: www.sewciopathgems.com

THE ART OF BEING A HUMAN BEING
by Matthew Nouriel

The year was 1985. I was with my mother visiting family friends in Brussels, Belgium. I had just turned 7 years old and I remember flipping through the television to find something interesting to watch. As I changed channels I stopped on a colorful screen with music playing and the most beautiful woman I had ever seen singing and dancing. It was the music video for Madonna's *Dress You Up* which was shot live at her *Virgin Tour* concert. I was totally mesmerized and I didn't want to take my eyes off of her. At the same time I felt compelled to dance -- and dance I did. Little did I realize then, that one channel switch would insert someone into my life who would influence me, comfort me, inspire me, humor me, and stand up for me for years to come.

As soon as we got back home to London, I told my dad I wanted a Madonna cassette and asked him if he could please buy me one. A few nights later he came home from work with *Like A Virgin*. I listened to it obsessively and learned all the words to every single song. Soon I became a bona fide Madonna fanatic trying to get my hands on any magazine article, any record or any picture of hers I could. I'd watch *Top of the Pops* every week hoping to see her videos. I plastered posters of her all over my bedroom walls. I even got in trouble with one of the Rabbi's at the orthodox Jewish school I attended for having a picture of a scantily clad Madonna in my school binder.

As time went on my obsession only grew stronger. By age 12 I owned every Madonna album released up to that point and was relishing in the media frenzy which surrounded her every move. Her song *Vogue* was in heavy rotation and newspapers were covering her *Blonde Ambition* Tour every day. It was all very exciting for me. What wasn't so exciting was the dread of having to study for and ultimately deliver my Bar Mitzvah, but what sweetened the deal for me was my trusty dad agreeing to take me to the *Blonde Ambition* concert taking place just a couple of weeks after my birthday as my Bar Mitzvah gift! She was scheduled for one date, July 20th at Wembley Stadium and I had to get tickets. The release date was announced but by the time I got through on the phone to purchase tickets, they were sold out. I was crushed, but within hours a second date was added! July 21st. I called again, and again it was sold out. Devastated. All I wanted was to get a chance to see my idol perform live in what was to become a groundbreaking game changer of a show, and it wasn't going to happen. Just as I pulled out my diary to scribble my barely adolescent emotions and utter devastation into it I got word that a third date was being added! July 22nd. I was going to get tickets if it was the last thing I did. I sat by the telephone and waited until the allotted time and then I dialed. Busy. Dialed again. Busy. Fuck! Okay. Stay calm. Try again. Bingo! The term "third time's a charm" has never been more true. I got 3 tickets to Madonna's *Blonde Ambition World Tour* '90 and nothing else in the world mattered anymore. I, Matthew Nouriel, was officially going to see Madonna live!

My Bar Mitzvah came and went (dance party, Madonna cake and all), and I counted down the days to July 22, 1990. Wembley Stadium did not have assigned seating, just an open field and the stadium seats around it, so we had to get there early and wait outside until the gates to the stadium opened. My dad, my friend Daniel and myself set out at 8 am for the adventure that awaited us. We got there and sat and waited. As the hours rolled on, the surrounding area filled with more and more people -- 72,000 people to be exact. Sometime in the afternoon we could even hear a sound check from behind the gates. My 13-year-old mind felt like I was living in a dream. Was this really happening? All those hours of waiting outside flew by like time was irrelevant, and it was. I was going to see Madonna live.

Sometime in the late afternoon the gates opened. I showed my ticket and attempted to sprint across the field to try and get as close to the front as possible but was yelled at by a security guard "No running!", much to my father's relief as he could not keep up with me and he didn't want to lose me. We got about a quarter of the way back from the front of the stage. We were instructed to sit on the floor and so we did. As the stadium was filling up, my dad was looking around and seeing the thousands upon thousands of people surrounding us and started to panic. He was fearful we'd be crushed in the crowd once the show started and so he insisted we go and find some seats along the perimeter of the field, which we did.

When the show began I lost my mind. Like, completely. It was an out of body experience. I screamed and cheered and sang along to every song. After the first few songs Madonna gave an impassioned lecture on the word fuck. "Fuck is the reason you are here. Fuck is the reason I am here... On the count of three, I want everyone to scream fuck!" I'd never seen such unabashed, unapologetic, sheer and honest vulgarity before. I reveled in it. It was so liberating, especially given the conservative culture I come from. Needless to say, I, along with 71,998 other people, screamed "fuck" while laughing hysterically at the urging of the Queen Madonna. The one person there who did not scream along was my father, who looked as if he'd just been slapped silly and was now in a state of shock. He just looked at the stage, then at the crowd, and then at me, helpless to what was going on around him. But that was just the beginning. After a couple more songs, Madonna now appeared in a gold girdle on top of a giant red bed with male dancers wearing cone-shaped bras on either side of her. She began a slow and seductive rendition of *Like A Virgin* and as the song went on she began simulating masturbation, first with the two dancers and then by herself. At this point it just felt a bit awkward watching this with my dad right next to me. I kept looking over at him and will never forget the look of utter dismay on his face, his hand over his mouth and face bright red. He never said anything or expressed anger over what we were seeing. I think he was just shocked, after all, in his day Elvis shaking his hips was considered a scandal. At the time I presumed he was furious. No one had ever gone as far as she did and I don't think anyone has since. (I later found out my dad's face was red because of all the hours we spent sitting in the sun!). The show continued and I continued enjoying every second of what was the most momentous occasion of my young life so far.

1990 was an interesting year. It marked my entry into adolescence, it was the year I had my Bar Mitzvah, and it was the year the world saw Madonna break through many social norms. Everything she did had an element of queerness to it. She would talk about the AIDS epidemic with compassion and without shame, she featured very queer dancers on her tour, she discussed homophobia in interviews, and she had been flaunting a friendship with the lesbian comedian Sandra Bernhard -- fueling rumors that they were in a relationship and rather than denying it, she played into it. I remember it being on the cover of the British tabloids every time she was with Sandra and so many of my peers at school saying they were no longer fans of hers because she was a "disgusting lesbian". Homophobia was nothing new to me. I had been bullied all through school for being a "poof", and here was Madonna trying to make a difference and seeing people now direct it toward her infuriated me. At the end of the year the video for *Justify my Love* came out which took her exploration of human sexuality to another level. The tabloids plastered the shot of her from the video kissing another woman on all of their front pages. It was all anyone was talking about, mostly negatively, but it meant something else to me. While everyone was going off about what a whore and a pervert Madonna was, all I could see was my idol -- this beautiful pop goddess whom I looked up to and loved with every fiber of my being -- was now telling me the secret I so desperately tried to keep hidden didn't need to be a secret. She was telling me that gay is okay.

  In 1991 my parents got divorced and that summer my mother moved me and my brother to Los Angeles with her to be closer to her family which had made their way there after the Iranian Revolution. One of the things I was most excited about was MTV. I relished in the day-long Madonna-thons they would have and would watch MTV News nightly for the latest on Madonna. I had missed seeing *Truth or Dare* (in the UK, *In Bed with Madonna*) because its UK release date was after we had already left, and unfortunately for me, by the time we got to LA it was no longer playing in theaters. I couldn't wait to see it and to relive my memories from the *Blonde Ambition* tour. I had started school in the 9th grade full of hope that I wouldn't be bullied or made fun of anymore since no one was going to know me. The American school experience was very different, I didn't have to wear a school uniform and I went to school with a much more diverse pool of kids. Unfortunately for me my hopes of being free of mockery were quickly gone. I don't know what gave me away but I suspect it probably had something to do with my first P.E. class when we were outside and a giant bumble bee type thing started clumsily flying around me and I jumped up and started screaming and flailing in complete terror. We certainly never had bugs like this in London! Add to that the fact that I was super skinny, super tall, had big hair, a funny accent *and* was queer (though closeted), certainly made me an easy target. Adjusting to life in Los Angeles was difficult and I didn't really have any friends for the first six months at school, so my only source of stability and comfort was Madonna. When Truth or Dare was finally available on video I ran over to the local Blockbuster store and rented it. I must've watched it 10 times in a row. Watching her and how brazen she was made me want to be brazen. She was bold, assertive, powerful, unapologetic, and these were qualities I wished I had. The documentary placed a lot of focus on her gay dancers, not in a positive way or in a negative one, but rather just showed them as human beings. She normalized queerness in a way I'd never seen before. Up until then the only portrayals I'd ever seen of gay people were negative ones. We were either sex crazed perverts who spread disease and were shunned by respectable society, or worse, the butt of jokes. There was no positive image of gayness back then, certainly not that I'd seen. The one moment in the film which I remember the most vividly was the scene where she and her dancers are playing a game of Truth or Dare and she dares two of the male dancers to kiss each other, which they do. I had never seen two men kiss before and I can honestly say that one moment on film definitely changed my life. I started coming to terms with my sexuality after watching *Truth or Dare* and I truly believe I wouldn't have been able to accept myself had it not been for Madonna and her documentary. Once I came out I became the butt of many jokes myself, just as feared, and though it hurt, I knew I wasn't the problem -- the people making the jokes were. Madonna taught me that. She taught me self-acceptance. She taught me to embrace my queerness and to celebrate the things that made me different from everyone else.

    As the years rolled on so did my admiration and appreciation of Madonna. I lived through every incarnation of hers in awe and with excitement. There was the *Sex* book era (where she pushed the boundaries of acceptable sexual expression even further), *Bedtime Stories*, *Evita*, *Ray of Light* -- and so much more all the way up until 2019's *Madame X* era. I'd been to almost every tour of hers and every single time without fail become that screaming 13-year-old fan all over again. Throughout the years I recall people constantly having something negative to say about what she was doing, criticizing and scrutinizing everything from her hair to her videos to her face to her body, and yet she persevered effortlessly and unbothered. Even now, as I enter my 40's, seeing how she rises above the way people speak about her age and how a woman over 60 shouldn't behave the way she does, inspires me. Watching her explore life through her art has set the example for me to do the same in my own way. To not be afraid to try different things and not be scared to discover new elements of my own psyche. She taught me the art of being a human being, and for that I am forever thankful to her.

JTranR01
@JTranR01

I just turned 19, recently graduated high school. Ran into a former teacher while buying. The cashier tried to shame/embarass me by showing it to my teacher, "Look at what he's buying." My teacher simply replied, "So what. He's an adult." She then smiled and wished me well.

10:53 AM • Oct 22, 2018 • Twitter for iPad

"I think Madonna has a great deal of intelligence and capability. I have a lot of respect for her. She's taken her career and maximized it with intelligence and creativity."

– Carole King

Dazzling Donna
Artist: Thea Emilie Eikeri
Instagram: @artby.theaemilie

FEMINIQUE
by Teddy Margas

I was a "feminique" child. Don't bother looking the word up, it doesn't exist. I made it up. It's a mash-up of feminine and unique. I was the portly kid who was always picked last for any sport. Unbothered I'd sit on the sidelines and daydream about being on ABC's *Challenge of the Network Stars*, a hit television program in the 70's that pitted celebrities from different network shows against each other. I'd imagine myself in my red Adidas shorts and matching tank top walking to the tennis courts for a game against Farrah Fawcett.

I never wanted to attend a concert or wear an artist's t-shirt the way my peers did. I always thought people should pay to see me perform, wearing shirts with my image emblazoned on it. What was my talent, you ask? I had no clue. I wasn't a dancer, I had been rejected from Glee Club, had no desire to be in the school band, yet I had dreams of being a big star.

Cut to several years later, I had excelled in theater and was able to make the class laugh. They couldn't poke fun of my weight or the 'girly' way I held my books if I did it first. Eventually, I had them all on my side and became quite popular. Isn't that what we all want in high school, popularity?

I heard her before I saw her. I had no idea what she looked like. She had this soulful R&B voice belting out a song called *Everybody*. "Dance and sing, get up and do your thing" became my mantra; I was hooked. I knew what 'my thing' was, I just couldn't articulate it. A low budget video was released for this song and I was shocked to see a small white girl with tousled blonde hair wearing the coolest distressed leather vest I'd ever seen. I remember exactly where I was, in a hotel room in Wildwood, New Jersey with my family. On the television was this video advertising this singer's appearance at the local club called The Playpen. I was too young to go but something clicked. Her name. Madonna. I thought that was the most brilliant stage name I'd ever heard. I was in love. I begged my parents for a cool, distressed leather vest for Christmas that year and had it come in a plus size I would have gotten it.

Funny thing this Madonna. I can place myself in the exact moment in time when I first heard each of her songs. I know where I was, what I was wearing, what I was doing, what I was thinking and what I was feeling. No other artist, no other human being for that matter, has been able to do this to me.

When I first started coming out I was spending a lot of time in New York City. I started seeing the world with brand new eyes. I felt a part of something, I was no longer relegated to the sidelines. My friend had an apartment in the East Village and we would get ready for nights out on the town, sipping house cocktails and listening to music. I was bedazzling a black motorcycle jacket with black rhinestones to wear that evening. Madonna was to appear on MTV's *Video Music Awards* that night and I couldn't wait to see her. The iconic performance of *Like A Virgin* started and I was glued to the TV. She wore a bridal gown and writhed all over the stage. I loved her. I could relate. My friend, a New York City theater queen, was in shock. "Who is this?" he asked, "She's a mess! She can't sing, she can't dance. She kicked off her shoes." I was furious. How dare he! I told him who she was and he said, "flash in the pan." I have haunted him with those words ever since.

Having fully embraced my homosexuality, I was in Key West Florida with friends dancing en masse at a T Dance. I was feeling cute in my denim cut off shorts, t-shirt and construction boots, when I looked up on the monitor and saw a very different Madonna. The set was very *Metropolis*. Gone were the rags in her hair and the rubber bangles. She looked like a movie star, surrounded by hot dancers who were sweaty, sexy gods -- all obeying Madonna's instruction to *Express Yourself*. Thank you Madonna, we are. We are!

I moved to Los Angeles to pursue stardom. The glitz and glamour of L.A. was intoxicating. When one wants to be famous the city of angels is the place to be, for fame and the lure of it is all around you. During the week I was taking classes: scene study, script analysis, improv, you name it. On the weekends I'd hit West Hollywood, the gay mecca, to dance. To escape. To be. Dancing on the floor at Micky's, an iconic West Hollywood nightclub, I heard the now legendary strings and my ears perked up. I was wearing my go-to 90's ensemble -- square cut lycra shorts, a sheer button-down shirt (unbuttoned, of course) and black combat boots with the laces removed. My hair was cut into a bob and it took mounds of mousse to give it that wavy, unattended look. I looked up at the huge video monitor and caught my first glimpse of *Vogue*. The images were what I was experiencing in my pursuit of the Hollywood dream and the words couldn't have matched my journey more. I was stunned. I couldn't move. I stood there on the dance floor with hundreds of others like myself, transfixed. Mouths agape, we were rendered speechless as we worshipped our vintage Hollywood Screen Goddess.

Never having been an athletic person I desperately wanted to become more fit and healthy. Inspired by Madonna's *Truth or Dare*, the concert film/documentary where we see Madge running with her bodyguards, showing her hotel gym to then-friend Sandra Bernhard and being the disciplined athlete Madonna was, I took up running. Off and on for several years I tried to be as disciplined as she was to no avail. Then the *Evita* soundtrack dropped and that was it for me. I felt Madonna's power. "There is only one man who can lead any workers' regime." I would chant this to myself during my runs and it made me unstoppable. I had heard the songs from *Evita* many times over, but having them come out of Madonna's mouth, they took on a very different meaning. A hunger for something more was evident in the way she sang these songs. I read that she lobbied very hard for this role and you can tell by listening to it. Set a goal and go for it. You'll be high-flying adored.

I was in love with him. I didn't know it at first, but it came to me one night as we worked together. He was perfect. Dark hair, dark eyes and a smile that could light up a room. He had an infectious laugh and I loved going out of my way to make him laugh. We shared the same love of house music and would hit all the after-hours clubs to dance the night away. The more we hung out, the more my love for him grew. Deeper and deeper. I wanted to tell him, but I didn't have the nerve. We were friends. Friends don't fall in love, do they? It's insane how one minute you feel one way about someone and the next you feel something completely different. I wanted to tell him so bad. Perhaps he felt the same way, perhaps he was afraid to tell me. We'd stay up late watching television and he'd fall asleep with his head on my shoulder. Tell him. Tell him. I couldn't. On one of our many nights out in a club, the DJ stopped the music. This had never happened before. In the middle of evening, silence. The lights in the club all turned blue. I looked at him and wondered what was happening. The music started again, only it wasn't a throbbing drum beat, it was violins and a deep bellowing bell sound. It was the beginning of *Frozen*. I loved this song, but hadn't heard this Victor Calderone version yet. The DJ mixed the haunting symphonic opening of the album version with this amazing dance mix. The club was washed in blue lights as the drumbeat swelled and then magic happened. It started to snow. In the club. On the dance floor. Snow. Well, fake snow, but it was unbelievable. I looked at him and thought, "if I could melt your heart." We were staring into each other's eyes in this frozen moment when he leaned forward and kissed me. To this day when I hear the first few notes of the song *Frozen*, I melt.

  Was all of this coincidence? How can one human being have such an effect on so many others? Is this Madonna's power? Is this her talent? Was this just a sign of the times? I don't know. I don't know if I will ever know, but I do know this…Madonna allowed me to be me. Unafraid. Unashamed. Unabashedly me.

Howlin' 4 Hoechlin
@rain20001

We should all have the balls to be ourselves. To ignore the insults. To be a little bit more like Madonna. Intelligent, driven, unashamed, and unapologetic. Besides, without Madonna a lot of people would have to find someone else to talk shit on. Thank you Madonna! #Madonna

10:03 AM • Sep 13, 2021 • Twitter for iPhone

"I say more power to [Madonna] though I don't know how much more power is out there."

– Carrie Fisher

Queen Madonna
Artist: Ben Philip
Instagram: @benphilip2002

IMMACULATE CONNECTION
by Heather Turman

"Why don't you have some sort of Madonna monument on campus?" I curtly asked the Secretary at Rochester Adams High School one hot August day.

"I honestly don't know... You'd have to write a letter to the Superintendent," she politely replied, though no doubt taken aback by my interrogation.

I grew up in a small town outside of Detroit, Michigan, and like Madonna I, too, had felt the oppressive energy of my environment. It was conservative, restricting – the kind of place where self-expression was a risk and it was safer to just blend in. I'd ventured to the site of Madonna's former high school that day to purchase some apparel -- partially because I liked the brown school color, but mostly because as a highly obsessed Madonna fan, I was more interested in representing her school than my own. But when I arrived at the site of Madonna's formative years and found no evidence of her past attendance – not even a simple photo to commemorate the institution's most successful graduate – it served as yet another reminder that the things I valued carried little importance in the Midwest, and it simply wasn't the place for me.

By the time I was born Madonna was already a household name, so I have never existed in a world she hasn't. She has just always been there, presiding over pop-culture like an omnipresent being, informing history and our lives in ways we weren't even conscious of. I was always drawn to her due to her ability to delight in a scandal, and even as a young girl I could tell that there was a definitive line between the people who liked Madonna and the people who loathed her. It always seemed to me that the adults I actually thought were cool, *also* happened to like Madonna, and that was important evidence for my developing mind. But it wasn't until 1998, when I was 11, that my super-fandom was solidified. Her video for *Ray Of Light* was playing around the clock on VH1 (yes, I was the kind of 11-year-old who watched VH1 instead of MTV) and there was a lot of hoopla surrounding her "post baby body" and how great she looked "for 40." I was flummoxed to hear this news -- I mean, my own mother was 40 and she sure as hell didn't look like *that!* My prepubescent brain took note and I decided then and there that when I was 40, I was going to look as good as Madonna.

That may have been the first time Madonna would inspire me to achieve something but it certainly wouldn't be the last. Her episode of *Behind The Music* premiered shortly after and I remember being totally captivated not only by Madonna's amazing rise from obscurity to superstardom, but by a simple sentence she said about her journey that resonated deep within me: "I just wanted to get the hell out of Michigan."

There it was -- hope. If Madonna had been able to ditch this small, backwards town for a big life full of excitement, so could I! I began studying every move she made and in a strange way, having grown up in a family that didn't identify with any particular religion, Madonna became mine. I was a member of Madonna's congregation and I took everything she said as gospel. I had always felt misunderstood, but when I listened to the things Madonna would say it was like the feelings I had about everything were articulated for the first time, and I felt seen. My connection to her was immaculate. My best friend in middle school was a member of the church, too, and she and I would emulate all of our favorite Madonna looks every chance we got -- even when it meant looking like a lesbian couple in matching pantsuits and ties (a la Madonna's photoshoot for *InStyle Magazine* circa 2001) at our school's Valentine's dance. We were outcasts whose bond was rooted in rebellion, and as our friendship blossomed, so too did our worship of Madonna. She became our savior who protected us from the prevalent small-mindedness and conformity of our peers and encouraged us to not accept mediocrity.

In celebration of Madonna's birthday one year, my friend and I baked a cake and put on her 1990's video compilation. We were innocently enjoying our Madonna dance-party celebration when my mom came home and accused us of being a lesbian couple. I mean, sure, we were best friends who dressed in matching gender non-conforming outfits -- but that didn't make us lesbians. And honestly, I didn't see why it mattered. In Madonna's religion, we believed in love no matter what. Still, my mom's accusation rained on our parade and I ran upstairs to my bedroom and cried.

Years later, after I had packed up all of my belongings and moved across the country to Los Angeles in my own pursuit of artistic expression -- I did come out as lesbian. My friend laughed and said, "God dammit, Heather -- everyone is going to think we were a couple back then!" but my mom had a less enjoyable reaction, refusing to see me for the next five years.

Truth be told, my mom hadn't been around that much in my formative years. Her parenting style was a little more laissez-faire, which in ways I'm grateful for, as it enabled me to harness a strong sense of independence -- but without Madonna to look up to, I could have started down a dangerous path of rebellion while chasing parental attention. But unlike other troubled teens who turn to drugs and other detrimental forms of coping, I threw myself into hard work and focused on my dreams. One thing Madonna always exemplified was the importance of self-discipline and how there was no greater drug than achievement, and so I adopted that same mindset. When I had no one else to guide me I looked to her and she showed me the way. When I came out as a lesbian and my own mother decided I wasn't worth accepting, I knew that Madonna would accept me no matter what and that gave me permission to continue to love and accept myself even after my family had rejected me.

Once I had settled into life in Los Angeles, I started doing stand-up comedy. Once again I found myself inspired by Madonna's influence. I talked openly on stage about being gay and utilized irony in my act to point out the hypocrisies of the patriarchy and sexual expression. At the time talking about going down on another woman was still considered taboo, but I didn't care. Madonna had taught me to express myself and not compromise my artistic integrity, and so I went full steam ahead. I performed in 20 States and 75 US Cities during those formative comedy years, and each show served as a form of therapy -- healing me from the pain that occurred when I had come out. Like Madonna said about her *Blonde Ambition* tour, it was cathartic.

It's now been over a decade since I came out and things have improved with my mom in recent years. She is much more accepting and our relationship has begun to repair itself, but I honestly don't know what would have happened to me if I hadn't spent my formative years studying Madonna. Her influence is embedded in every fiber of my being, her guidance present in every move I make. I certainly wouldn't have moved across the country to pursue artistic endeavors, nor would I have found the strength to come out or share about my experience on stage. Madonna brought me here, to this place. And one night, she almost brought us together.

I have had my fair share of close-encounters with Madonna. The first was when my friend and I saw the *Re-invention Tour* in Chicago. As any real fan knows, Madonna can't stand when people sit during her shows – and I mean, how could she? She's up there doing the unthinkable in several-inch-high stilettos every night, giving all of her energy to us – and lazy concert-goers can't even stand in one place for a few hours to show their appreciation? Blasphemy! Alas, my friend and I were the only ones on our feet in the first ten rows in Chicago. We were literally leaping out of our seats and dancing with joy, so when Madonna took a moment to introduce *Crazy For You*, she paused, pointed in our direction and said, "...because I'm crazy for *you*!" And we literally lost our shit.

The next close-encounter was during the *Rebel Heart Tour* in 2015. I had recently sold a screenplay so I had an abundance of money in my Madonna ticket fund and planned to spoil myself. However, since ticket prices for the first few rows had hit $13,000(!) in LA, I had to look at surrounding cities and eventually scored a front-row seat in San Diego for one-tenth of that price. The moment I took my seat I knew I would connect with Madonna that night. Surrounded by screaming gay men, I stood out like a sore thumb with my mousey Midwestern-ness and my homemade t-shirt, so when Madonna came over to our section and scanned the crowd, I could see her sizing me up and wondering what I was doing there – after all, I certainly didn't look like her usual fan. All the gay men stuck their hands up, desperate for her to bless them with her touch. She slapped several of them, but she stopped at me and didn't slap mine. Instead we locked eyes for a moment and I just smiled, holding my own, and it was like she knew she didn't need to bless me with her touch, because I was already blessed. When I tell this story to people they roll their eyes at this statement, but anyone who has had the distinct honor of looking Madonna in the eyes would know it was true.

Recently, after the COVID-19 pandemic rendered live stand-up comedy obsolete, I found myself in need of a quick job and got one at a fairly posh, upscale restaurant in LA where many celebrities frequent. I joked to a friend that Madonna had recently purchased a home not too far from the restaurant, so maybe she would come in one day. Then, one night, I was out at a comedy show called *Cosmic Joke* – and Madonna actually did come into the restaurant where I worked. Of all the restaurants, in all the land, Madonna had come into mine… and I wasn't there to meet her. Talk about a *cosmic-fucking-joke*! While the little girl inside of me mourned the experience of a run-in with her one-true idol, the woman I am today knows that the environment of a restaurant, where I served tables, was not the place where I desire to make Madonna's acquaintance. In fact, that job had become increasingly toxic and began to take its toll on my well-being – and the appearance of Madonna felt like a sign that I had to get out of there. While there is nothing wrong with serving tables, and it's something I've had to turn to several times throughout my life as an artist, I couldn't help but feel like I had taken a step back – like I should have been on the other side of the table. *Fuck, I was worthy of being on the other side of the table.* So, shortly after that divine intersection, I quit my job and got back to my creative endeavors. Madonna may have simply ventured out for a glass of rose that night – but she managed to show up just when I needed her, to remind me of my power and guide me back to my righteous path.

Like Madonna I grew up outside of Detroit, Michigan. Like her I craved an escape from the oppressive environment I was raised in. I followed in her footsteps and fled as soon as I could, and today I, too, am an artist who stands for love and freedom of expression. Her demonstration of fearlessness helped me to overcome adversity and her radical self-love helped to shape me into a person I am proud to be. While there may not be a commemorative monument of Madonna outside of Rochester Adams High School, there is one within me – deep inside my rebel heart.

Tess Barker
@TesstifyBarker

We are nearing our 4th decade of not giving Madonna enough credit!

10:13 AM • Feb 20, 2019 • Twitter Web Client

"I would really, really, really like to be a legend like Madonna. Madonna knows what to do next, and when she's performing, the audience is just in awe of her."

– Britney Spears

Material Girl
Artist: Jacqueline Bissett
Website : JacquelineBissett.com

MY LIFE AS MADONNA
by Denise Bella Vlasis

It was the summer of 1983 when all of the sudden I began to hear the comments "oh my gosh, do you know who you remind me of? You look like that girl on MTV," and "you look like that singer, Madonna." I had to run home and flip on MTV to see what all this was about. And there she was, in all her beautiful blonde glory, this incredible blue-eyed girl slithering on the ground singing to the camera with an intense piercing energy that absolutely captivated me. This is the girl people were comparing me with? She had recreated Marilyn Monroe with an edge and was doing it so much cooler than I ever could have. I didn't think I looked like her, but I did recognize an energy, a spirit, a determination in her eyes, and a balls-out, unapologetic way about her that I completely identified with. I really felt some kind of kinship when I looked at her. Yes we were both Italian-American, both dancers, both girl drummers with hopes of "making it", but it felt deeper to me. Perhaps we had been soldiers together in another lifetime, or many lifetimes. I knew I felt a connection to her that I could not explain and wanted to know more.

In these days, I spent hours a day in dance class or searching through Drama-Logue magazines for any kind of performing work. I was hungry to perform and would send out headshot photos to anyone and everyone who would open my mail submissions. I stumbled upon a casting notice from a production company searching for a Madonna lookalike. I wondered if this was something I could pull off since so many people started calling me Madonna. I even had a pretty well-known casting director tell me to "lose the Madonna look" to get more serious acting jobs. With absolutely no costume or idea how to *be* Madonna for this audition, my mom helped paint the iconic mole on my face, threw together a makeshift costume and made the long drive up to Hollywood to the audition. I felt so lucky to have her support and confidence.

When we got to the audition there was a room filled with faux celebrities -- Lionel Ritchie, Tina Turner, Cindy Lauper, and Michael Jackson. I panicked thinking I was way over my head with this level of talent. I looked at my mom who gave me that 'go for it honey' look she always gave me. When they called my name to audition, I jumped onto the stage and with all my heart did my best to try to lip sync a song that I barely knew and tried to recall that magic of Madonna in my mind. "Do you know any other Madonna songs you can perform for us?" called the casting lady after my performance, to which I replied, "Sure - what song do you want me to perform?" knowing right well I did not know any other Madonna song. The casting lady popped on the song *Burning Up* and I thought to myself "what would Madonna do?" so I pulled up all my steps from dance class and mixed in some rolling on the floor and realized at that moment, I was willing to do whatever I had to get this role. Well, I booked the job and the director gave the advice to "learn how to really be Madonna" -- and with that, my journey and dreams took a change of direction.

Being Madonna was far more education and therapy than I could ever have anticipated. Madonna made no apology for who she was, how she performed, or what she believed. Inside of me, I was not that brave. I was painfully shy, insecure, scared -- a people pleaser with fears of judgement. But when I stepped into my costume, put on the make-up, painted on the mole and became Madonna, all of the fear disappeared. When I was Madonna, I was fearless, a lioness ready to pounce, kicking down doors of Hollywood and no longer feeling inadequate. I discovered a new sense of self-esteem and confidence only Madonna could bring. I believe it was this confidence that made casting directors stop and notice me and the job offers began to roll in faster than I could accept them. Suddenly all of the dreams I had growing up were coming true. People from newspapers, magazines and TV shows wanted to interview *me*. It was bizarre and surreal that suddenly with this armor of Madonna I could somehow be somebody and for the first time in my life, I felt special.

I still had doubts of trying to become a "regular" actress or if it was even possible to keep working as Madonna. Should I listen to the casting guy who told me to look less like Madonna? Is it possible to manifest more work looking like her? Could I utilize my likeness for more work opportunities? As fate would have it, a video editor, Luis, saw my headshot and called me about a contest on MTV held by Madonna. We were supposed to make a video to Madonna's *True Blue*. I told him I would put something together and get up to Hollywood ASAP so we could film something. He was very skeptical of "just filming me as Madonna," but I begged him to at least look at me through the lens of the camera before he decided to quit. He picked up his camera and with a crappy little boombox I began to perform for him. I could feel his energy shift and his excitement. We had twenty-four hours to film, edit and submit to MTV. We ran from Melrose Ave to Fairfax in Los Angeles with costumes flailing everywhere, often changing hair and outfits behind a car or store. During our shoot, Luis became discouraged as we ran into at least three other girls dressed up like Madonna also filming themselves for this contest. I giggled to myself when running into other Madonna wanna-be's out on the streets, this was something I dealt with often, but confidently knew my tribute to her was different from other girls. I spent countless hours really learning how to bring the best parts of her to life with absolute love and integrity. I told Luis not to worry about others and to stay focused on me. I stayed up with him for 24 hours to edit the best parts and make sure my lip-sync was on point and facial expressions accurate. We were able to get our video into MTV by the deadline and when Luis called MTV to check, they said they had literally "thousands of videos submitted" and they would get back to us. About three days later, we got the call that we made it into the contest and we were the only Madonna lookalike picked. Luis was excited for this news as this could greatly help with his career, but for me, all I wanted to know was "Did Madonna see our video?" to which they replied, "Madonna picked her top ten." This was the only validation I needed to make a decision for my future -- I would move full steam ahead impersonating Madonna as a career.

With a successful performing career spanning over 28 years, I went on to book every kind of job that would have never been available to me as just a blonde actress. I traveled the world performing live on stage. There were giant billboards of me dressed like Madonna displayed all over Asia. I worked on many television shows, music videos, print ad campaigns, and voice-over roles as Madonna. I worked as a stand-in for Madonna, a body and parts model, and even a decoy as her. I met so many famous people because of their love of Madonna and always had incredible conversations. I even booked a commercial *with* Madonna for MTV (talk about full circle). I got to meet Madonna, perform as Madonna, and MTV production even hired me to help them with the other costumes and Madonna eras. I went on to write two books, start an agency and train other inspiring performers to begin a career as a celebrity lookalike.

How could anyone have dreamt what has unfolded in my life, thanks to one courageous, pioneering woman who dared to do things her way? Madonna taught me how to rise above the ordinary and dream bigger. I happened to be a dancer on American Bandstand the day that she said she wanted to rule the world, and I never forgot her words and belief in herself. Madonna has blessed my life with not just opportunities to perform, but she has grown inside of my soul to remind me to stand in my own power, to be resilient, stand up for what I believe, not listen to the haters and keep making art. It's okay to be provocative if you have something to say -- it's okay to be strong, sexual, outspoken, out of the box, and unapologetic for what lives inside of us. She has helped me look with new eyes at ageism and challenge the norms. Like Madonna, I am not defined by my age, my past or what others view as failures. I am present and continuously learning and as long as I am still living, I will still be creating.

Living life through the eyes of Madonna has been an adventure like nothing else. I have met movie stars and politicians and have been to high profile parties and events. I have heard stories of hundreds of people who met her or wanted to meet her. I have been catered to and received more attention than I should have. I have been idolized and hated. I have received praise and have been spat on in the face. I have learned what fame feels like without ever being famous. One can only imagine what the real Madonna experiences in her everyday life -- and this is why to me she will always hold her title of QUEEN.

sohox
@Sohoxo

Thanks for all, Madonna, your are an inspiration for many of us, I love your heart, and all that you give me all this year's with your songs, after 18 years listening you I've learn to think different about life and love, I've learn to love myself and others, thanks you for all, M.

3:29 PM • Aug 6, 2020 • Twitter for Android

ABOUT THE EDITORS

Raised in Texas, **LeeAnn Tooker** is an actress, comedian, and writer. Her comedy album, *In the Room*, is available for download and/or streaming on most major platforms. She currently resides in Hollywood, California fulfilling the dreams of her 9-year-old self.

Heather Turman is a comedian and screenwriter. She co-wrote, produced and starred in the feature film *Stuck* alongside Joel McHale and Heather Matarazzo, which is available now on most major platforms. She lives with her wife, their four animals, and plenty of Madonna memorabilia in Los Angeles.

Get your exclusive "**Madonna Fans Do It Better**" t-shirt at etsy.com/shop/MadonnaFanShop.

SPECIAL THANKS

We are grateful for all the Madonna fans that came together to share in this tribute to the Queen. Below is the complete list of our contributors.

Gerardo Alvino
Tess Barker
Patty Bourrée
Jacqueline Bissett
Matías Alejandro Cabrera
Faye Rapoport DesPres
Thea Emilie Eikeri
Joshua Flores
Amber Gignac
Lisa Gopman
Saima Huq
Alan Bennett Ilagan
Juan Manuel Gutierrez Iñiguez
Lance Lockhart
Teddy Margas
Heather Matarazzo
Gabriel Méndez
Ignacio Miranda
Nick Musmecci
Tommy Natoli
Matthew Nouriel
Ben Philip
Jamie Tran Reitnauer
Matthew Rettenmund
Lawrence Stern
H. Louis Tooker
LeeAnn Tooker
Heather Turman
Maria Antoinette van Schooten-Krzeminski
Denise Bella Vlasis
Patricia White

Printed in Great Britain
by Amazon